TidalWave!

Getting Rich Fast in Network Marketing
with
The Eight Secrets from the Asian Masters

Dedicated to Vicky

Other products by Edward Ludbrook

100% Success Basics
100% Confidence
How to Coach
How to have a Fantastic Year in Network Marketing
100% Motivation
100% Leadership

Published with permission by:

Sound Concepts
782 S. Auto Mall Dr., Suite A
American Fork, UT 84003

For additional copies of this book or other titles by Ed Ludbrook visit us online at
www.100PercentTools.com

First published in New Zealand by 100% Success Institute Ltd,

ISBN 0-9582554-7-4

Foreword

From the days of the Silk Road, the Asians have been well known for their entrepreneur spirit. It is of no surprise that the Asians are able to accept and develop the Network Marketing industry wholeheartedly.

In TidalWave!, Edward masterfully describes the secrets to creating momentum and a massive income in Network Marketing. This TidalWave! strategy is true. It is the only way people make it big in this business.

His approach to the industry is practical and his coaching helped grow our company by 3000%. This book will enable a person who is willing to Learn to ultimately achieve success in Network Marketing.

NH Chua
Asian Network Master
30 year industry pioneer

'Most people stumble over opportunity yet pick themselves up and walk off as though nothing had happened'.

Winston Churchill

Preface

Since 1994, my passion has been finding solutions to the challenges facing people in the fast growing Networking industry.

Firstly, like many others, I struggled explaining why Network Marketing was the 'hot' industry for the future. After strategic analysis, I published my 'Big Picture' presentation that has been used by over one million people from Iceland to Idaho to explain why this industry is 'the' place to be!
I hope you will get the chance to read the NEW version of the book called '100% Confidence' as it reveals why Network Marketing has evolved and entered a dramatic new growth era based on a new business strategy.

Secondly, I wanted to help people create higher levels of success in the easiest way possible. Through a simple strategic shift to competence based learning and coaching, everyone now has a 100% chance of Success, [thus it's called 100% Success Strategy.] It creates the foundation for explosive lasting growth. The book is called 100% Success Basics.

My greatest challenge has been finding out how to help new people grow their networks faster. New people are the lifeblood of our business and techniques that will help them produce faster bigger results will drive the industry.
My second major challenge was to fix the low activity rates which was creating high failure and confidence issues.

Slow growth is the nightmare for all new people as it creates slow income growth. It crushes their belief in the income opportunity.
It has been my mission to find the answer to this, our greatest challenge, and learn how to create a TidalWave!

Have you ever had a situation when moving away from a problem helped you find the answer faster?

A few years ago, I took an opportunity to work in Asia, the fastest growing region of the world. The Asian Network Masters are producing incredible results and I wanted to discover their secrets.
Working with these dynamic Asian leaders from Hong Kong to Indonesia, made me realise EVERY successful leader I have ever known in the world employed the same network building strategy when they built what I now call a TidalWave! Building a TidalWave! is the key to success in Network Marketing. It is simple to understand and thus success in Network Marketing is in the grasp of everyone who wants it.
I hope this book helps you build your personal TidalWave! I hope it helps you exploit this once-in-a-lifetime opportunity and helps you to GET RICH QUICK!

Introduction

'Get Rich Quick!

I love this sentence!
Few sentences create as much hope.
Few sentences create as much scepticism or scorn.
It makes people nervous even talking about it.
Our newspapers, magazines and conversations are peppered with the stories of those who have defied the odds and got rich quickly.
We like to call them 'lucky'.
We have created the massive lottery industry based on the dream of hitting the jackpot and never having to worry about money again.
Personally, I hate the lottery. I have never played it. What masquerades as a 'bit of fun' actually feeds the belief that getting rich is beyond the abilities of most people. That getting rich is based on chance. It undermines people's ability to dream.

What is a Get Rich Quick scheme?' a man asked me from the back of the room.
I was teaching the staff of the British Advertising Standards Authority on how to recognise pyramid scams from valid income opportunities, such as Network Marketing. This was an honest question which reflects the ignorance of most people towards making money.

'That is a great question' I replied, 'there is a lot of confusion over so called Get Rich Quick schemes. Traditionally, they are illegal scams yet I think we should all try and understand what drives so many people to get involved in the whole area of alternative income opportunities. Think about it, everyone wants to get rich!
Being rich means you have more choices to have a better life. The only questions are How? and How fast?'

If it took you five years to build a business that made you rich, is that quick?
When you consider that most people work for forty years only to retire on half the income they struggled to live on before, five years is very fast, thus a Get Rich Quick scheme should be a goal of everyone.
'Most people believe that getting rich quick is impossible. Their teachers, parents, and the media told them so. This is why they are sceptical about Network Marketing. It breaks the rules. **Average people can get rich quick.**
Incidentally, the reason they can is simply that this is a growth industry that uses human capital. If it relied on financial capital, then the people who control money would get rich. The billionaires and bankers.

It will continue to boom because it is the ONLY industry where the average man can legally and honestly get rich QUICKLY.

Want to be a millionaire?

If you are [still] reading this book then I assume you want to get rich quick. Bravo!
Rich is possible.
Rich to me is not billions, a private jet and mansion.
Rich to me is financial security AND a lifestyle to enjoy it. To not worry about money. For most people, its more than a US$million but not a lot more.

So what are the chances of being a millionaire?

In 2003, Newsweek magazine estimated that there were three million US$ millionaires in the USA and probably another three million elsewhere in the world. Six million millionaires! There is a lot of money around.
Obviously, being a millionaire doesn't have the lifestyle it did 20 years ago yet it still provides a high level of financial security that the other six billion people in the world do not have.
One in a thousand. [six million in six billion]
Take out three billion abject poor in China, India, South America, Africa. Take out one billion children, the uninspired, the seriously ill and the odds of getting rich start tumbling in your favour.

You can get rich. You just have to learn how.
This book will help you learn how.

Making a million

Across the world, people are realizing that the greatest opportunity for them to make money quickly is through Network Marketing. It is the one opportunity for the average man to acquire the success system and it is still booming. I am just disappointed that some people do it so badly.

For years, I have related in my industry speeches at conferences across Europe, the incredible growth statistics from the Asian region. Of the millions joining and sky-rocketing sales. Asian networkers get rich faster than others in the world.
Surprisingly the power behind the Asian phenomenon comes down to one concept which I call the TidalWave! This TidalWave! concept focuses peoples minds to create explosive growth. To harness the power of people.
To create this growth, these Asian Masters have developed Eight Key Techniques or Attitudes, which I call Masters Secrets.
They are simple yet powerful.
They can be used all over the world. You can use them to grow your business faster. Master them and you will double or triple the growth in your business.
Use this book to Get rich quick!

Edward
The Network Coach

How to read this book

This is an instruction manual for those starting in Network Marketing. I have not used a lot of jargon or assumed any deep knowledge.
I want you to understand the TidalWave! concept and then learn some basic actions that have been proven to create the most successful Network Marketing businesses in the world.

The best way to learn from this book is to firstly, skim read the pages, scanning the headings, key points and recommended actions. Get a feel of the book.
The first section on creating a TidalWave! to Get Rich Quick is vital. You must understand this concept. You will realise how simple this business is and it will build confidence in you. Then read the Masters Secrets one at a time. If need be, re-read them so you understand their basic recommendations.

Lastly, take action.
Massive action.
Nothing of value occurs without action.

Contents

1. Join the right industry
2. Join at the right time
3. Have the right business
4. Take massive action

How to get rich QUICK!

The success stories of very rich people reveal that four elements must be in place for rapid wealth to be created. Those elements are:

1. Join the right industry
2. Join at the right time
3. Be in the right business
4. Take massive action

Seems simple enough, doesn't it? Be in the 'Right Place at the Right Time' and then work like crazy.

Right Place, Right Time

My '100% Confidence' book explains the facts why Network Marketing is booming and the future potential of the industry. If you haven't read it then I advise you to do so. The continual growth in this industry confirms its conclusions thus we can assume that this is the right industry to join today. I cannot judge if you are involved or offered a great Networking company. There are some fantastic ones around at the moment. Given that you have a great one, it is more than likely that for the first time in your life you are in the 'right place at the right time.'

Learn the system

All successful companies are based on a system. Making steel, software, selling clothes. The industry does not matter. There is always a system.
This is especially true in Network Marketing as the system is the power. By following a system, we can offer everyone an opportunity to join and make money.

All successful networking companies have a great system for you to follow. It will outline the steps you need to take. It will show you how these steps relate to their compensation plan and how you make money.
This book will not explain that system or recommend a different system.
The key to getting rich quickly is the way you work that system. This is what separates those who slowly plod along making income levels they are not happy with and those who are making fortunes.

The key to getting rich quickly is the way you work that system.

Don't be stupid

The skill is to learn the system well. If you can do this, why wouldn't you go into **Massive Action**?
How often in your life are you going to be in the Right Place at the Right Time with a System that you can learn to make money fast?
Once? Twice?
I will remind you of that Winston Churchill quote of early pages. Most people stumble on opportunity yet do nothing with it.
If you don't grasp an opportunity to get rich with both hands, you have got to be stupid. It's a tough statement. You might not like this word 'stupid' yet if you do not seize an opportunity to become a millionaire, to become financially secure, then you must be at least a bit 'stupid.'

The search for success?

In my early days, I noticed most new people were totally ignorant of even basic information as to why the industry was growing and thus had little confidence in a long term career.
They had small goals, low motivation and no answers to those sceptics who wanted to rubbish their new opportunity. It was therefore not surprising that my 100% Confidence book answering those concerns was so successful. It creates what is called 'Inspirational Confidence' which boosts action in NEW people.

Building confidence through skills

The other reality was that so many new people either took no action OR stopped quickly after starting so we must build their confidence through becoming competent in skills.
We have to create 'competence confidence' which is the key to massive action because people 'know' they can succeed [100% Success].
The biggest challenge is simply that 98% of people will not learn skills or build confidence on **without proper competence coaching**. I call this **100% Success Coaching** and you can learn the basics in just 24 hours on www.risingstarsecrets.com.
Learning skills through 100% Success coaching is the key to sponsoring, confidence, motivation, activity, productivity, independence AND residual income YET it is NOT the key to getting rich.

Learning skills by 100% Success coaching is the key to everything in Network Marketing EXCEPT getting rich!

The Key to Getting Rich

Everywhere I have gone in the world in this business, from Iceland to Indonesia to Idaho, the following is true; those that have become leaders, those that have got rich, those that have got rich the fastest, ALL have created what I call a TidalWave! to start their business.

This is the Magic Formula to getting rich quickly.

Create a TidalWave!

Definition:

A TidalWave is a huge first growth wave which creates momentum in your business

To understand how to create a 'TidalWave', you need to understand some fundamental concepts.

Income Curve

Everyone, I repeat, EVERYONE, must learn the following graph of how network income grows in Network Marketing. The power of a network income is that it is about a lot of people doing a little bit. The more people you have in your network, the more money you make.

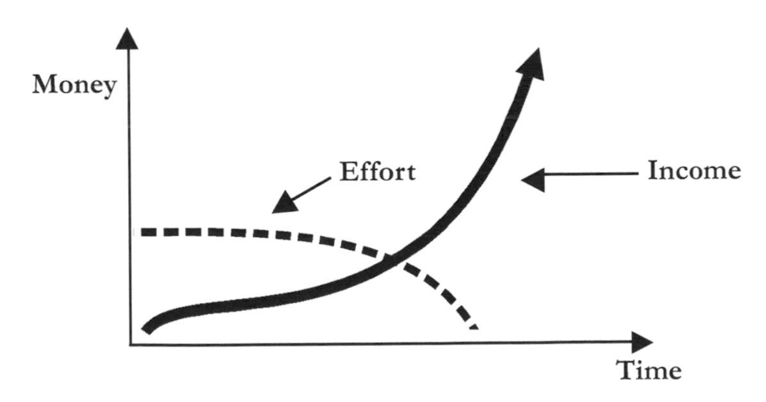

Effort stops, income continues

At the start, you have to put the most effort in and your income is the smallest.
Do you know any business or career that does not start like this?
Here is the exciting part, eventually, if you have built your network properly, your effort can go to zero and your income will keep growing.

As a friend of mine says 'at the start we are over-worked and underpaid, and at the end we are underworked and over-paid!'

LESSON

The most effort is invested at the start

Why does it keep growing?

A network will keep growing after you stop working because it is using the Geometric Power of Numbers. I discovered a great Asian story explaining this power;

One day a prince was inspecting his lands when he came across a peasant playing chess. Thinking he could not lose, the prince challenged the peasant to a game and said 'Beat me and I'll give you whatever you want – fine clothes, a feast, a palace.'
They started playing and as normal in stories, there was an upset and the peasant won. The prince says 'what do you want?' and braced himself for the price of losing – only to hear the peasant ask for rice.
'Put one grain of rice on the first square of this chess board. On the second put two grains, in the third put four grains. Double the grains for each square of the board' says the peasant.
The prince laughed and readily agrees, because being royal and being a parable, he is stupid.
He orders his Rice Keeper to put the rice on the board. Only to find he is ruined. There are 64 squares on a chess board and if you double a grain of rice 64 times you end up with more rice than in all of India [nine trillion trillion grains!]

What happened next?
I don't know. In reality, the peasant was probably hanged for making a fool out of a prince yet we have all been taught a valuable lesson about the power of numbers.

LESSON

Use the Power of Numbers to get rich

Increase the Factor

Once you understand the Geometric Power of Numbers, the next step is to understand the power than 'increasing the factor' would have on your income.

1

2

4

8

16

32

Keep doubling, like the grains of rice and eventually the numbers grow into big numbers. Remember on a chess board, there are 64 squares.

Network Marketing taps into the power of numbers because everyone in the business follows the same business system. By following the system, everyone is able to duplicate actions and introduce more people. Now the concept of earning a little from a lot has power.

You may only earn $1 per person so $1 times 32 is not very exciting. Keep doubling and 32, 64, 128, 256, 512, 1024… Now the income is interesting, yet not exciting.

When it doubles from $16,384 to $32,768 per month, you are very excited.

But you had to double fourteen times!

What if we had increased by a factor of three?

By adding just 1 more at each level, instead of 32, we get 243 AND there are over 300 more in the total.
LESSON – Produce the highest factor possible

With a factor of 5, there are 3,000 more! If this was people in your team, this would be $3,000 more per month in income.

1				
2	➔	**3**	➔	**5**
4		**9**		**25**
8		**27**		**125**
16		**81**		**625**
32	➔	**243**	➔	**3,125**

It is very simple…**Sponsoring more people increases the factor!**

Theory versus reality

In eighteen years of experience working as the Network Coach with countless organisations, I have seen numerous ideas, concepts, tips or techniques to make it big in this business.

Not one of them truly described what I know [and other leaders agree] is the reality for those that make it big.

Theories or success stories are useful and inspiring yet they do not explain what is ABSOLUTELY VITAL.

The theory is that your network income grows in an ever-increasing income wave. The curve takes time to grow yet when the power of numbers takes over the income curve arches up as your network explodes. Much like a snowball rolling down a hill gathering more speed and size.

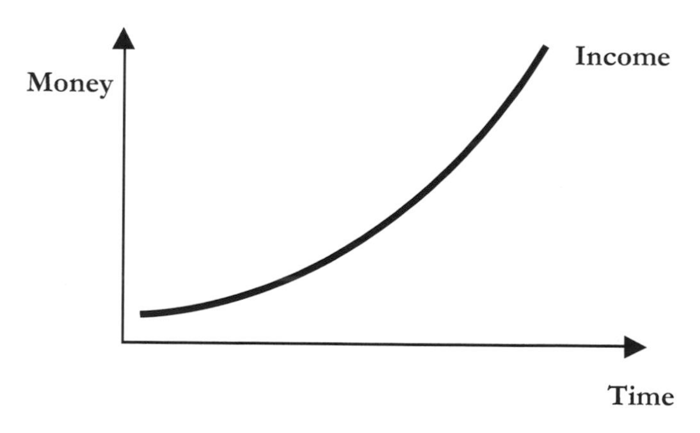

Income grows exponentially.

The reality is that your income grows in a series of growth waves. Each wave requiring a new strategy, hard work to get going and then a period of momentum when it grows with little effort on your part.
Eventually, the momentum dies and your income stalls. You then adapt your strategy and give your network another hard push to start the next growth wave. The bigger the network the easier it is to start the next growth wave.

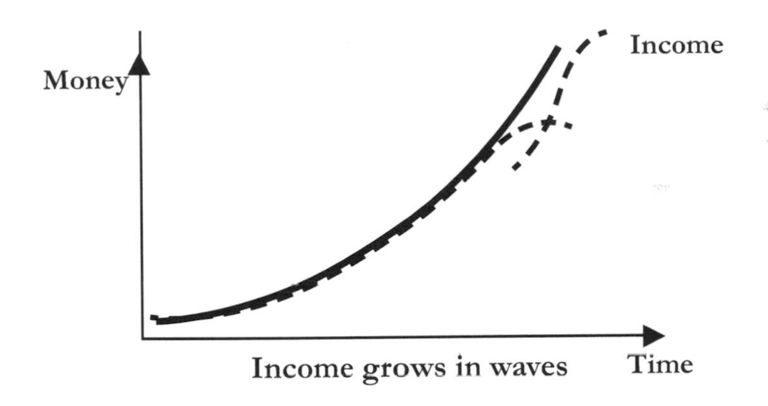

Income grows in waves

The most critical growth wave is the first. ONLY those people able to create momentum in their networks EVER earn a leadership income. It is the only determinant of success or failure.
THUS the lesson for everyone who joins this industry MUST BE....
Your objective when you join is to create MOMENTUM in your network.
You need to create a strong first growth wave. To be sure of success, that first growth wave must be a TidalWave!

Vital Belief!

You must accept the following reality...all great opportunities can grow fast. They can have explosive growth. Your income can double every three months for three years!

Because Networking employs the power of numbers, it can grow fast. The industry is still very new. The age of your company is irrelevant, the opportunity for growth is endless.

Too many people believe [or want to believe] that slow growth is normal, natural or expected. This is wrong and self-defeating. You can create explosive growth fast. Believe this and take action.

What is success?

You cannot hit a goal if you don't know what it is!

What is 'success' in Network Marketing?

What an important question!
Research shows that if you ask this question of Networkers and you will get a whole range of answers such as 'achieve my goals', 'create residual income' or 'achieve financial freedom'.

These answers may seem correct yet there is too much variation and lack of clarity. Presented this way means that you cannot define success.

The fact is that you CAN define 'success'.

The fact is that you MUST define 'success'.

But why MUST we define success?

You must find a definition of 'success in your business' so you can determine IF you and others can be successful.
The only way people will sponsor their warm market or take the action necessary to succeed if they KNOW people have a very high chance of success. They need '100% confidence in success' or they will never invest the time, money or effort required to succeed. I call these people risk-averse 'Intrapreneurs' and they are 98% of all Networkers.

Become a TEAM Leader

To discover the definition of success it's normal to look in the wrong place. Rather than looking at the rewards from your business opportunity, you need to be looking at the business opportunity itself!

Remember this is a 'franchised systemised' business so the company who created your business opportunity will have decided what they consider as 'success'.

If you look at your compensation plan, you will see that there is a rank/title/position where the company shows that they think that you have been successful as a Network Builder. This is the first level that <u>they begin investing</u> big money in you in the form of 'leadership incentives'; travel, car plans or bonus schemes.

This is when the company believes you have reached the MINIMUM level of success as a business builder. I call this position a '**TEAM Leader**'.

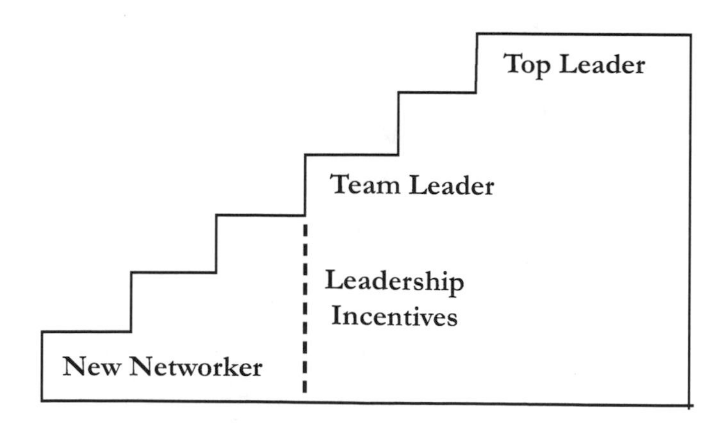

Minimum Level of Success

Remember this in NOT the maximum success level, just the start. It is the level that they believe everyone can achieve. A level they have 100% Confidence in 100% Success.

Major performance goal – **I want to become a TEAM Leader.**

How to get to TEAM Leader

Every TEAM Leader position in every Networking company on the planet requires you to build a team through producing Numbers of people.

This is how our business works; you make 'a little bit from a lot of people!' You need Numbers. And to get Numbers you must create Momentum.

SUCCESS = TEAM LEADER
TEAM LEADER needs NUMBERS
NUMBERS needs MOMENTUM
MOMENTUM = SUCCESS

Achieving Momentum determines
if you are successful or not in this business

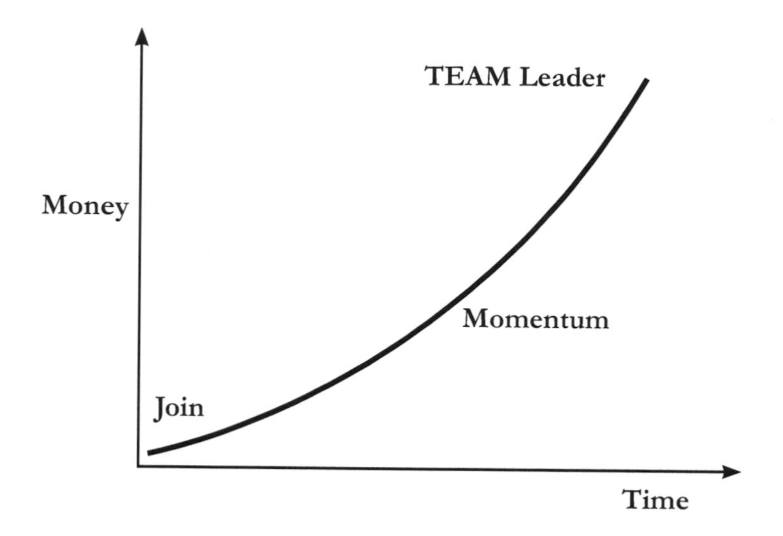

Everyone can become a TEAM Leader because Everyone can learn the skills and create momentum.

First wave is key!

What happens in reality is that when a new person starts, depending on a number of factors including their motivation, time and confidence, they will attempt to build a network. This will mean they will sponsor people and coach them to do the same. One of the following things happens:

1. **Small wave – no momentum, start again**
2. **Half wave – no momentum, a base to build from**
3. **TidalWave! – momentum, enjoy the ride**

1. Small Wave

For whatever reason, you either did not sponsor enough people or were unable to coach them to duplicate your efforts. They create a small growth wave like the graph below. Their network is small and not naturally growing. The main reasons are:

- Your Networkers did not learn the basics of coaching so had little confidence.
- You never discovered the <u>true motivation</u> of people to find the fire in them.
- The <u>system was unclear</u>, too complex or out of date so the people became confused or lacked confidence.
- They <u>did not work the system</u> even though they understood it.
- They expected results <u>too soon</u> so stopped before time.

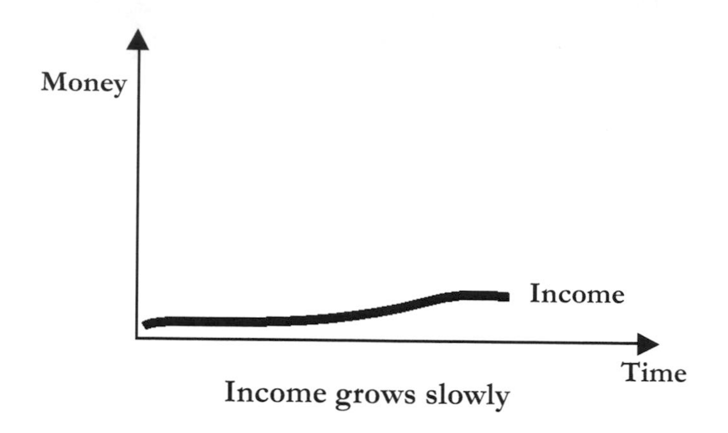

Income grows slowly

Creating small and slow results is so demotivating most people will give up or just focus on customer profits. You will hear a lot of excuses blaming or justifying their lack of results. Should they give up?

Maybe.

They may feel exhausted, frustrated or humiliated.

Yet they must still have the same desires as when they first joined. The motivation inside must still exist so they must still be looking for an opportunity that will satisfy their desires. Considering that they are in the right place at the right time, it makes the concept of quitting a poor option.

All you did was 'false start.' Do not worry, many people false start. They just did not quit.

Recommendation

Go back to basics and start again. Use the experience and improved skills to create a new explosive start. Do not creep, charge!

2. Half Wave

A Half Wave is when you are making progress yet it is slow. Like the graph below, your team grows YET the pace of income growth will never create the fire and the motivation for a large network.

The network does not go into MOMENTUM, which is when the organization grows without your help. A slow build network will never get you to top leadership positions.

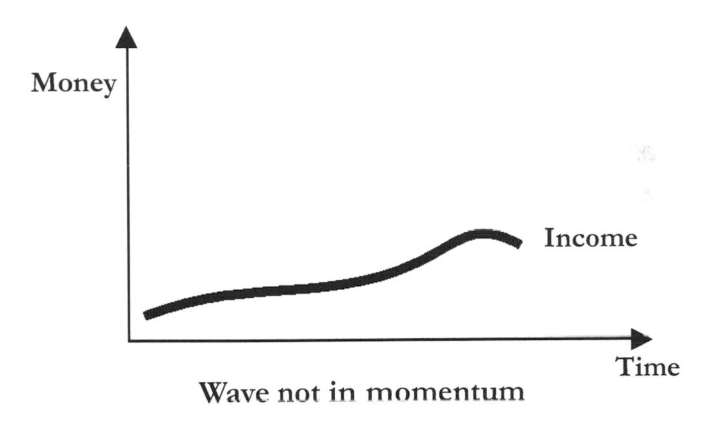

Wave not in momentum

Why do networks grow slowly?

There are many reasons.

Low confidence producing little action is the main reason. They may be hesitant in action. They may be procrastinating. They may not be used to helping people.

Some people are happier with slow growing networks. It makes them feel more in control. It allows them to build 'loyalty, teamwork and skills'. All are vital parts of a long term business YET the reality is that slow growth does not create Momentum.

The best a slow growing network will produce is a small stable income and a base to build a new growth wave.

Recommendation:

What happens if you have a slow growing network?
You have a base of people yet they may be tired. Hard to inspire as they have not experienced fast dynamic growth. They need to see others create explosive growth before they get excited again so stop: Take a breath, Regain your energy. Examine the way you are working: Are you creating an environment for fast growth? What are you doing that is slowing the growth?
Then find a new inspiring message [a new development in your company;. A new product, country launch, incentive or programme.] Use this message to drive new growth.

TAKE THE LEAD!

You must take the lead and start sponsoring quickly. Feed the new positive rapid success stories to your other people to help them build their confidence and excitement again so they can go out and sponsor and build fast as well.

3. TidalWave!

Some people create a first growth wave that enters what is called MOMENTUM. This means their network starts to grow without their effort.
Each week more members join the business. Each week, sales climb. Instead of creating a growth wave, you create the initial surge and the MOMENTUM creates the TidalWave!

With rapidly growing sales come rapidly growing income. This creates excitement whereby emotional energy takes over. People step outside their natural conservative comfort zones and go into MASSIVE ACTION!
Suddenly people who claim they have no time for anything new, make time for the opportunity.
Suddenly, people who would not join any income opportunity, get involved. This enthusiasm is contagious. And so is the fear – the fear of lost opportunity. Many people start to join for they fear that they will miss out on the 'next boom company'.
This is MOMENTUM. It is the most powerful drug in all business. It is the feeling of the invincible army.

The key to success is the initial surge!
You join, learn the basics and then go into MASSIVE ACTION sponsoring people and coaching them to do the same. Get the Power of Numbers working quickly for you so as to increase the expansion factor - **Sponsor lots of people fast**.

The key is the TAKE OFF! point.
Surfers have to TAKE OFF. They paddle as fast as they can to get enough speed to ride the wave.
A rocket has to TAKE OFF to get into space. The greatest effort is made at the start to break the bonds of gravity.
To be successful the key period is the TAKE OFF!

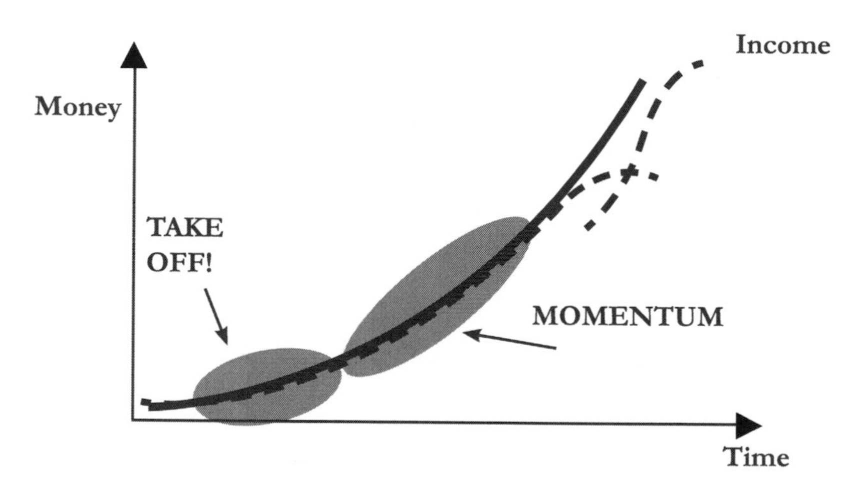

The TidalWave!

The Take off requires massive action.

He built a TidalWave!

A billion dollar Network Marketing company was launching in Europe and I was invited to have breakfast with Tom, one of their top leaders, in the Dorchester Hotel in London. He earned more than US$3million per year so I thought it may be fun to meet him. His story confirms my theory as he said;

'I may earn $3million per year yet I have not worked my business for years.'

He had my attention!

'What is your secret' I asked. Tom continued.

'For the first two years in the business, no-one worked harder. I would get up at 5am to talk to my leaders on the East Coast [of the USA] who were a few hours ahead of me and I would go to bed at midnight after talking to those on the West Coast who were behind my time zone.' My efforts created such excitement and momentum that my network eventually grew without me. Without any effort on my part, much of our global network is in my business. Now my job is to attend the launch of any new country.'

'Tough job', I thought looking around the dining room of the 5 star hotel.

His income had grown three times in the six years AFTER he had effectively retired. He was rich because of his massive effort at the start. He created a TidalWave!

Take-off point

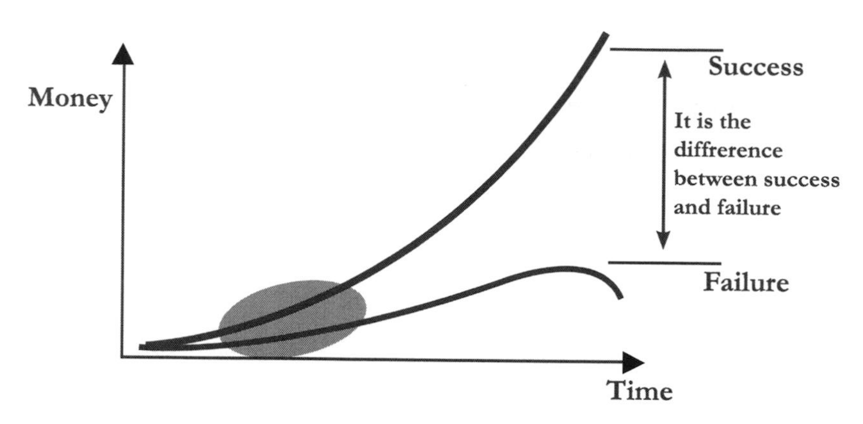

The difference is the Takeoff.

The difference between the Half Wave and the TidalWave! in terms of network size, income and enjoyment is more than huge. When you consider that there is a new growth wave after this one, the difference over time is monumental. EVERYTHING is about the early period.
This is the work time.
This is when you have to gain speed in your network. Like a rocket taking off, most of the effort is expended at the start to get the rocket in the air. Like a long jump athlete, a javelin thrower, an aeroplane taking off. Physics and the laws of nature continuously reveal that success is based on massive effort at the start.

TidalWave! is the difference!

The difference between winning and losing in Network Marketing is the TidalWave! The difference is purely Momentum.

The person who creates the TidalWave! is no better, no more experienced and had no more contacts. They just work a lot harder at the start. They grasp the opportunity given to them and do all they could.

Everyone is able to create a TidalWave! Everyone.

Simply follow the advice of the person who sponsored you into the business and go into massive action!

Don't think you can create a TidalWave!?

Concern at being able to create a TidalWave! is normal and expected. A lack of knowledge and skills will always undermine confidence. Anyone can succeed when success is based on following a simple system with the coaching of successful people.

You may have been in the business for a while and not been able to create a TidalWave! Do not worry!

All you do is to act as though you just joined and build a new network. I have seen it happen many times. You benefit from your experience. Once your team starts to grow, your confidence will rapidly grow.

So how do you do it?

The most important skill is sponsoring. Driving what I call the Flywheel. **The Flywheel creates the TidalWave!**

Definition:

A TidalWave! is a huge first growth wave which creates momentum in your business

Creating the TidalWave!

It is simple to create a TidalWave!. You may not believe it yet it is. The hard part is just doing what you are told and having the positive attitudes necessary to succeed [most people have dominant negative attitudes.]

What to do?

Your job is to rapidly grow a network. To grow it as fast as you can until others in your team catch fire and build their teams without needing your support [even though you may want to help].
This means that you are sponsoring people and coaching them on the system so that they in turn are sponsoring and coaching.

Two skills: Sponsoring and Coaching.

Momentum is based on adding new people to your team so Sponsoring is critical. The challenge is that 98% will not sponsor effectively UNTIL they have the confidence that those people will succeed.

This is why all new people MUST understand the basics of Coaching FIRST. This takes less than 24 hours to learn this is on Rising Star [www.risingstarsecrets.com].
Then the focus is on sponsoring and then coaching those need people on the skills. It is a process you can learn and follow.

Confusion, attrition AND gravity are the three enemies of momentum

Unfortunately, natural forces of human nature, **Confusion, Attrition and Gravity**, will slow sponsoring speed and destroy your chance of Momentum.

Confusion

Confusion kills confidence. A confused person takes little or no action!
It is important that when you explain your 'system', that you do it in a way that is not too detailed or is incomplete.

If your business is explained in a way that is too detailed then people wonder where to start or if they will ever succeed. You must learn how to explain the business simply.

If you explain your system too simply or if the system is incomplete then someone may take action quickly. The problem is that they will stop working after a few weeks as they discover they are missing the 'whole story' and get confused.
SOLUTION: **Coach them properly and there will be no confusion.**

You overcome confusion through 100% Success Coaching

The biggest source of momentum-killing confusion is not knowing how to coach properly. If you do not know how to coach a new person, your lack of confidence will rapidly be passed onto your new person and they will stop working.

Attrition

'Attrition' [churn or dropout] is the loss of people within an organisation. For whatever reason, they decide to stop working their business.
To create momentum, your sponsoring must be much faster than your attrition. In simple language, you have to add new people much faster than people are stopping.

Your Momentum Team

Momentum will created by the 'active' Networkers in your business. 'Active' means that they are actively sponsoring or coaching. If they become 'inactive' then this is called attrition. It is important to know exactly who are active and who are not so you can focus your valuable time and effort only on your Momentum Team.

Natural Attrition. There will always be a 'natural attrition' in your business. People will stop for a myriad of reasons. Accept it.
Speed is the key!

Excessive Attrition is attrition created due to something

that you are doing [or not doing]. It undermines confidence, motivation and productivity. Your business can either fail to achieve momentum or fall out of momentum.

Excessive attrition is the reason why a network will BUST after a BOOM. The simple solution is coaching! It fixes this problem immediately.

Coaching Kills Excessive Attrition

If you do proper coaching, you will NOT get excessive attrition. You will be 'close' to your people so will discover and fix any problems. Coaching will also boost productivity.

Speed is the key!

Natural Attrition only causes a problem in your team if you are growing too slowly. If your network is only sponsoring people at a slow rate then all you will do is replace the people you lost [your natural attrition]. You will never tap into the Power of Duplication.

To achieve Momentum, your business must be growing much faster than the natural attrition.

Gravity

100% Success Institute does research into many subjects and we ran a survey asking 'what is the main challenge you have motivating people?'
The Top answer was 'natural negative emotions' and the Number 3 answer was 'the negative opinions of friends and family'.

Natural negative emotions and opinions are like Gravity, a natural force, that can stop your network 'flying' with Momentum.
These emotions kill optimism, create skepticism and make you procrastinate when you should be working. They create the excuses and the justification for a lack of action. They raise questions about the potential of this opportunity to dull the excitement.
The negative emotions of 'Gravity' can slow your growth so much that the Attrition has the power to stop you creating Momentum.

Gravity and Attrition work together to destroy network growth

Overcoming Gravity

The best way to learn to overcome gravity and thus overcome the power of Attrition, is to think of other man-made things that fly. An airplane or a rocket ship. An airplane does not naturally fly into the air, the force of gravity keeps it on the ground.

The only way it flies is by using another law of nature to overcome gravity.
By gaining enough SPEED in the TAKEOFF the airplane taps into the force of aero-dynamics and thus is able to fly.

When is the most ENERGY used in an airplane flight? In the TAKEOFF to overcome the force of gravity. It is speed that overcomes Gravity.

You have to Takeoff

In Network Marketing, 'speed' is sponsoring speed. It's getting the Flywheel to spin fast enough to Takeoff.
To overcome the negative emotions of 'gravity', you use more powerful natural inspirational forces. The excitement of freedom. Of wealth and the time to enjoy it. Of a 'Desire' for a better life.
If you truly believed in this force,you would be working as hard as possible.You would invest the MAXIMUM ENERGY today. You will take MASSIVE ACTION AND URGENCY!

Urgency and Action communicates Belief

By applying maximum energy, you will communicate an URGENCY of action that will be felt by people. Urgency in business is unusual as it means either crisis or massive opportunity. In this case, you will naturally communicate that you have a fantastic opportunity. You will build people's BELIEF about the power of your opportunity to change their lives. They will start to believe they truly can 'Get Rich'.

Do It Now!

Making the Decision

The only way you will TakeOff and pioritise the business enough is to MAKE THE DECISION that you are going to create momentum.

It's a big decision!

The TAKEOFF period will be months of hard work. You will have to give up any non-priority things.
As the Asia Masters say 'you will have to have a FULLTIME' attitude. You can still have jobs and businesses Yet for the period TAKEOFF, as you are creating momentum, you must focus on your business.

I am not ready!!

If you are not ready to make the decision to go into the TakeOff period to create momentum to become a TEAM Leader and be successful [get the logic?], then that's ok and normal.

You need to build your confidence so that you KNOW that you can succeed IF you were to make the decision.
This simply means you are in the CONFIDENCE PERIOD and your job is to learn skills and build confidence. Obviously you will be able to make money and have fun YET don't expect to achieve income goals!!

The LOGIC...

- To succeed as a Network Builder, you must achieve the TEAM Leader position.
- To become a TEAM Leader, you need Numbers
- To get Numbers, you must create MOMENTUM
- To create Momentum, you need to TAKEOFF! 24/7 all-out massive action.
- To commit to the TAKEOFF effort, you need to make a Decision
- If you are not confident to make the Decision, then you are in the CONFIDENCE Period and focus on learning skills

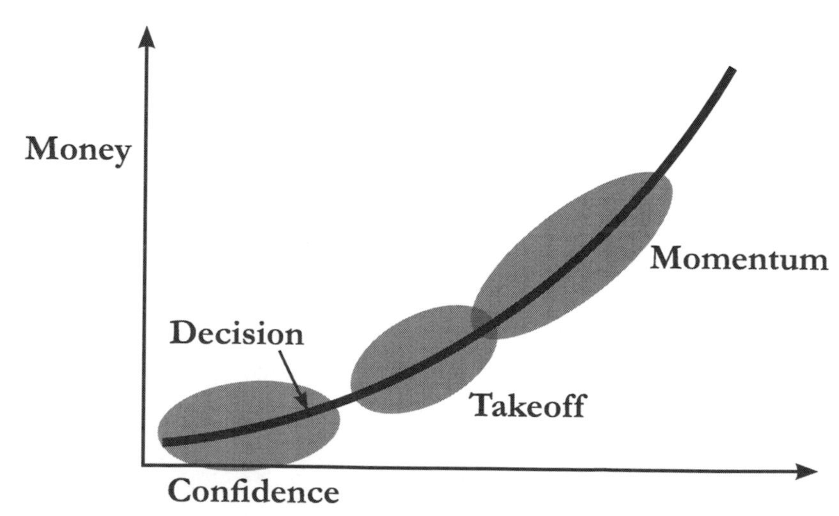

The Flywheel

It is a cycle. A wheel. The faster it spins the more people sponsored.
Nearly every successful network system has at its core a Rapid Growth System like the flywheel below.
The faster the Flywheel spins, the more people will join. The more people will get excited. The harder they will work. So the key is Sponsoring speed.

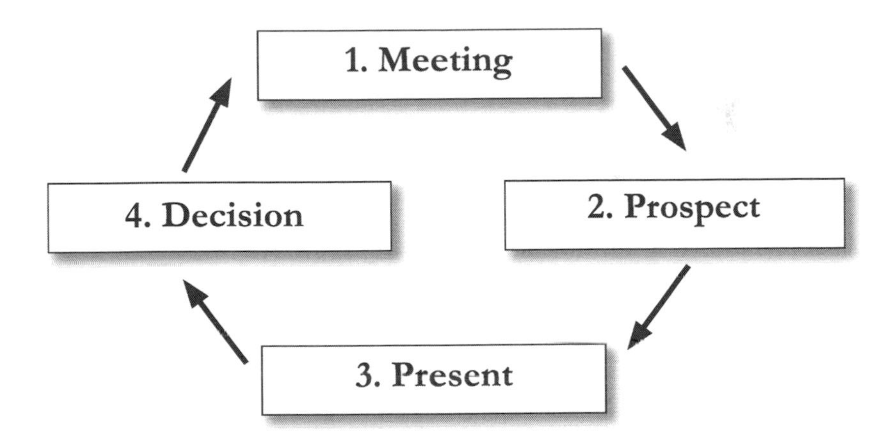

Step 1 – Meeting. Someone joins your team. Now for the initial Coaching Session. It is often called something like 'Quick Start', 'Fast Start' or 1st Step training/meeting. In the meeting you will cover subjects such as basic administration, knowledge and skills to get you prospecting, your 'story', goals [especially Learning and Activity Goals], contact list and coming to events.

Step 2 – Prospect. Talking to people, to find those who want to hear a product or business presentation. As many as possible. As quickly as possible. Enthusiasm is the key. Your sponsor should help you.

Step 3 – Present. Make business presentations to prospects. The more presentations you do, the more people will join.

Step 4 – Decision. Answer questions. Ask people to join. Follow up on those that are not ready. Some will join and some will not.

For those who join, help them start the cycle at Step One.

Is this all?

Absolutely not.
If customers are not serviced then no-one will make any money! Anyone who does not expect themselves and their teams to actively move products to customers is doomed to failure.

Your ability to create a Coaching/Skill development culture in your team will determine the strength and longevity of your network.
Skills create confidence. Skills create independence. Your goal is to create a confident independent network that will grow without you.

The magic formula

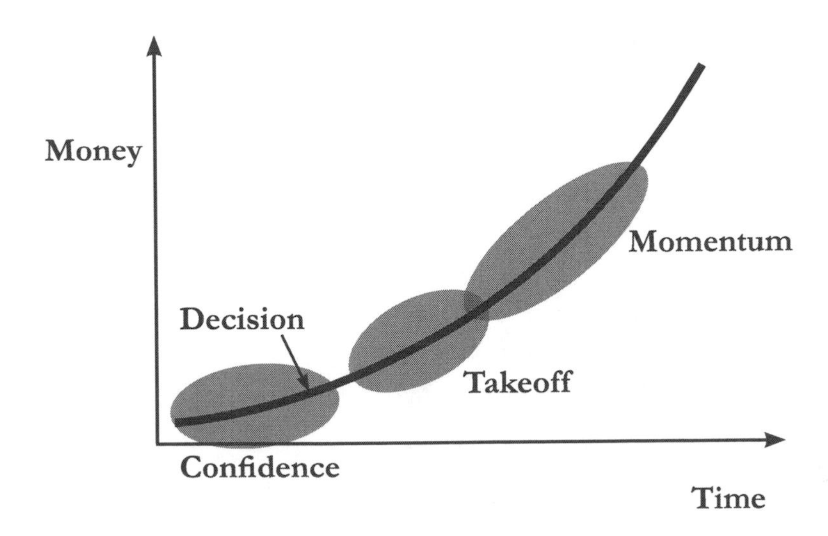

This is the magic formula.
First you need to take Massive action on the Flywheel to create a TidalWave! And actively coach your team to develop SKILLS for confidence and independence. They will build your business that will make you a FORTUNE.

The key is the TidalWave!
Your action. Your enthusiasm. Your inspiration and the results it creates will draw people into your team. The people who join will be inspired to work hard. To follow your lead. Is this simple? Very. Anyone can understand this. Anyone can learn this.
If you produce a positive, enthusiastic attitude and follow the advice of your sponsor then you will find it easy.
If you have a negative, criticizing, procrastinating, critical

attitude and do not follow advice or the system then I guarantee you that you will find it very difficult.

Masters of the TidalWave!

In the last ten years Asia has created extra-ordinary growth. Millions have joined at a rate not matched anywhere in the world. I have been fortunate to learn first-hand, how they have become the Masters of the TidalWave!

Magic Formula:

Take Massive action on the Flywheel to create a TidalWave!

Tsunami!

Tsunami : [Japanese]: ***A very large ocean wave caused by an underwater earthquake or volcanic eruption.***

A Tsunami is the Japanese name for the huge tidal waves created by underground earthquakes that sometimes strike their country. This word is now used across Asia for Tidal Waves. I find this ironic given that Japan is the most successful country in Network Marketing.

Asia is now recognized as the most dynamic region in the world and this is especially true in our industry. For years I have revealed the Asian growth statistics in my speeches across Europe and they confirm Asia as the new Masters of Network Marketing. They are Masters of the Tsunami! And look at these statistics from the World Federation of Direct Selling Associations!

- Millions involved. Asia has added 10 million people in just six years. Of the thirteen countries with more than 1 million involved in the world, eight countries are Asian! They are Japan, Korea, Taiwan, The Philippines, Thailand, Malaysia, Indonesia and Australia.

- Fastest Growth...In six years from 1997-2002, the America Direct Sales industry has grown by 24%, Europe has grown by 65% yet Asia has grown by 80%.

- Percentage of the population. USA has 5% involved, Germany and the UK have less than 2%. Taiwan has 20% of population involved! Korea has nearly 10%.

- Continued growth. ALL Asian countries grew in sales revenue and people involved last year.

- Biggest potential. Mainland China is considered the biggest new market when it opens in 2004. Numerous companies have already started and it is predicted that ten million will join the industry in the first three years. India could match this growth. Add to this the massive populations of Indonesia, Thailand and the Philippines.
  At the current rate of growth, Asia [excluding China and India] will have TWICE as many people involved in Network Marketing in 5 years! Include predictions for China and India and the numbers go off the page.

The graph on the next page plots the number of people involved by Region [Americas, Asia and Europe] from 1997 to 2002. Using the current growth rates, it predicts the industry size in five years. America grows steadily, Europe keeps booming and Asia skyrockets to over 60million people.

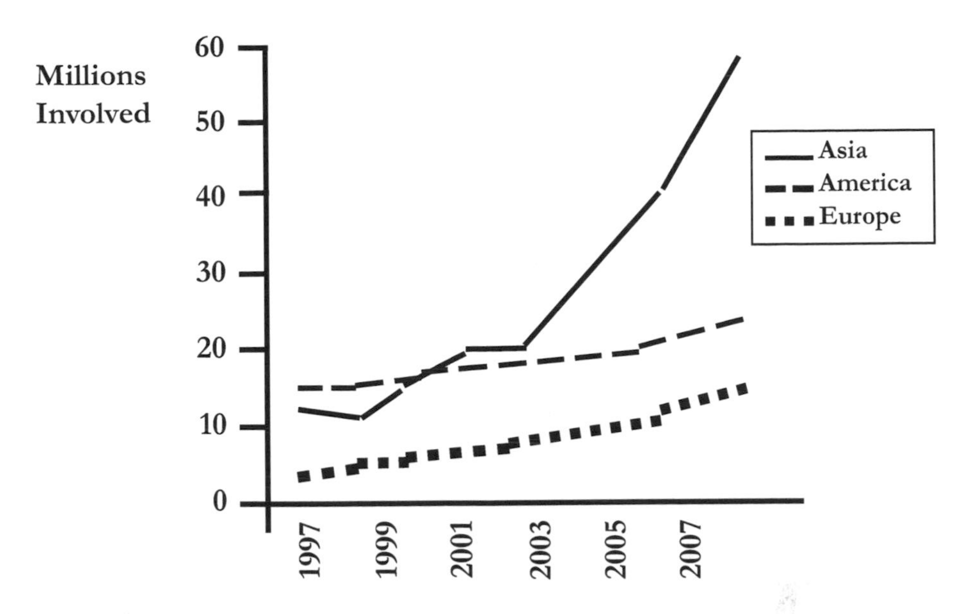

Industry leadership

For sixty years, Network Marketing/Direct Sales industry has taken its leadership from the USA. The new success stories and expert tips should now originate from Asia.

For this reason, I have spent four years working across Asia, discovering why these markets are growing the fastest. You can use these secrets to explode your business wherever you live.

危機

The Chinese symbol for crisis is made up of two symbols; danger and opportunity. Many people join Network Marketing when a crisis hits their life. They want something new. They want a better life. The danger is that they will approach the opportunity in the wrong way!

The Master's Secrets

What are the Asian Master's Secrets that you can learn to create your TidalWave!?

In the 1990's, Network Marketing in the USA exploded based on the use of new technology, such as direct ordering, audio cassettes and conference calling. Therefore, it is natural to assume that the Asian Masters must have a new tool, an improved technique or strategy.

Perhaps they have new markets, new products or just are a more entrepreneurial race of people who need an opportunity like this because they cannot get other jobs. Yet this is not what I found.

For a start, the Asians are actually at a disadvantage in most areas of the business.

- Asian markets are actually <u>mature markets</u> with many more Network Marketing companies operational than in other regions of the world. In Malaysia, there are 750 government registered Network Marketing companies and they consider that there are another 1500 unregistered companies! ***Everyone knows of Network Marketing so a sponsoring pitch based on a new industry will not work. They have also heard of countless 'new' strategies or systems so it is very hard to create excitement.***

- The middle class in Asia [the traditional driving force of Network Marketing in the world] is educated, employed, busy and relatively well-paid. ***They have many options so Network Marketing has to compete aggressively to win their attention and time.***

- There have been many pyramid scams that have caught the overly enthusiastic ***so most people are skeptical of Network Marketing.***

- There were ***no special product issues driving the market.*** Asians are educated on health, beauty, home, technology and family products. Product prices are not cheaper. The retail sector is very competitive.

- ***The distribution of products is more difficult.*** In fact in many countries, companies have to set up regional distribution centres as the mail can take over a week!

- Standard mass-market sponsoring tools such as brochures, CDs, audios, are ***rarely used.***

- Communication is harder with expensive slow mail and ***no communication technologies*** such as voice messaging or conference calling. They are mobile phone crazy!

- Places to <u>advertise</u> for new people are rare or non-existent in most Asian countries.

So the Asians do NOT have an edge in markets, products, distribution, systems, marketing tools, technology or advertising. All of the normal growth drivers are NOT available to them. So how are they creating such an explosion?
The answer is obvious…
The Asian Masters work the basics of Network Marketing better than everyone else!
It's that simple.
Not the flashy technology based networking - basic people networking.
Talking to people face to face.
Inspiring them to act.
Coaching them to learn.
Leading them.
Doing the hard work when it is required with an attitude that inspires rapid massive action.

The natural way of things

I find that Taoist philosophy helps explain why the Asians Networkers are so successful. As a philosophy based on the natural way of things it helps explain the behaviour of millions of people across many countries.
Taoism is an ancient spiritual philosophy written by Chinese sage Lao Tzu in his teaching Tao Te Ching, How Things Work. Its principles are still used by leaders across the world to understand a myriad of different situations.

To understand why the Asians are producing the fastest results, I find that the Taoist law of opposites explains how the Western focus on tools to help make communication more effective may make it worse.

Opposites attract each other

The Taoist principle of Opposites says that ***'all behaviour consists of opposites'***. The more you do of something, the more powerful will its opposite appear. Thus the more I strive to become beautiful, the uglier I become. An obsession with living reveals a fear of dying.

The natural form of communication is personal communication. Talking face to face with someone. We find it so simple yet it is actually highly complex as we communicate with our words, the tone of our voice, our facial and bodily expressions.

We have recently experienced a boom of communication technology. From mobiles to the Internet. All designed to help us communicate more effectively.

Conversely, the Taoist would say that we have created the opposite. They would show that whilst the quantity of communication has increased, the quality has decreased. There is less personal communication. There is less true communication. Valuable communication. They would show that we are losing the skill of truly communicating with people.

Personal communication is the true power of Networking. We have a unique business system that can reward people for personal communication.

It is the first in history and thus it is uniquely powerful. We can be the first and most powerful to communicate our message over all other businesess. Therefore anything that undermines or eliminates personal communication will undermine the power of networking business.

The Asian have no edge in products, markets or technology. They create superior results through attitude and action.

They focus on the basics.
They focus on personal communication.
They put all of their efforts into creating a TidalWave! as soon as they possibility can.

It was this discovery that prompted me to write this book because the Asian masters showed me through their actions [words are tough when you do not speak their language] what were the important basics.
Now you can learn their secrets.
What they think are the important basics.

The Asian Master's Secrets

The important lessons in life and business are always simple. They should be able to be used immediately. The Asian Network Marketing Masters used the same systems, used the same skills and had the same opportunities as everyone else. They just focus on different aspects. They have different attitudes. They take more action.

Lesson One	You need to explain a huge future that inspires massive action immediately
Lesson Two	You need total commitment to create a FULL TIME attitude
Lesson Three	You must form win-win relationships
Lesson Four	Everybody needs to hear about the opportunity as soon as possible
Lesson Five	Understanding creates the confidence to act with pride
Lesson Six	At the start, 24/7 effort is the minimum
Lesson Seven	Unquestionably follow the coaching of your Upline
Lesson Eight	Reward and recognise as much as possible

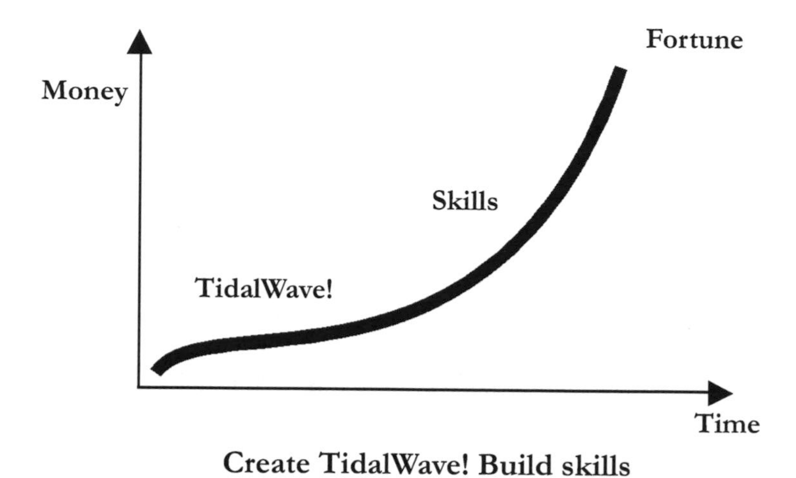

Create TidalWave! Build skills

Lesson One

You need to explain a huge future that inspires massive action immediately

They had just grown their team by 100% in one month so I thought it was a bit humorous that I had been flown into Malaysia to see how I could help them grow even faster.
In a room full of Chinese-speaking leaders, I first asked that someone do their standard Opportunity Presentation. I had seen the standard presentation slides created in the International Headquarters so I could focus on the presentation technique rather than the content. What I then saw amazed me!
For the next 45 minutes I got an amazing show of energy and passion supported by a slide presentation I had never seen. The presentation was full of pictures and colour. There were graphs and photos of official looking documents. Even though it was in Chinese I couldn't help but be inspired by the show.
'Give me the application form' I shouted at the end.
'I'm in!'

In traditional respectful Asian style, the leaders would not tell the international [and European] management that they had not designed a presentation for the Asian market. They just created their own.

The presentation was not a subtle mix of lifestyle pictures. It was information. Facts. Statistics that PROVED that this company was going to be HUGE. And anyone who joined NOW had the chance of getting seriously rich fast.

Asians sell it BIG!

They sell riches.
They sell opportunity.
They attempt to create a vision of their business that will inspire and excite the listener. This is why they need the facts. They use facts, statistics, gurus, official documents, etc to reinforce the credibility of the story they are telling.
They weave photos of the company headquarters, management, leaders and their team within the story. It becomes a visual and verbal feast of enthusiasm and opportunity.

Hype, you cry!

Everywhere I go, I hear people proudly claiming that their business doesn't use hype. Hype is exaggerating the potential of your opportunity. It is deceiving people. Hype is wrong yet I have found that, normally, these people have the most boring and slowest growth businesses.

People are confusing hype with great excitement or enthusiastic promotion. They want to turn down the music and turn up the lights.
Forget it!
We are in the advertising business.
Our job is to promote our products and opportunity over the noise of the marketplace. We need to use lights, sound, credibility and most of all the emotional messages that come from people's stories.

Every company does this. Go to a Microsoft or Coca-Cola conference. A film opening. The launch of a new pharmaceutical drug. Its all music, lights, film, professors and inspirational speakers enthusiastically promoting the POTENTIAL of the product or company.

The Asian Masters do not compromise on the presentation they present for prospect people to their team. They sell it big!
They do not compromise on the presentation materials; both corporate and personal. It is now just second nature for leaders to get photos with their new people to put in that new persons presentation. They get copies of any official documents to put in presentations. Even documents like export certificates. Anything that will impress to sell the business BIG!

Talk Cash

Asians talk cash. Money. Income. They show it. They explain how to get it. They know that this is the main reason why people join this business.

Too often I hear people focusing too much on the other benefits of joining this business. The training, friendship, independence, etc. Asians focus on money. Money, money, money.

This is why they are the fastest sponsorers in the world! People want money. First and foremost. They will get excited about the other benefits AFTER they start earning enough money.

Do you get nervous talking about money? Perhaps this is because you have never earned much money. Do not worry. You are explaining potential. Not making promises YET you must explain big money and talk about a big opportunity.

Master's Lesson

People get rich in this business. Millionaires. Many people earn more money than they ever believed possible. A month's salary in a week. So tell people that this is possible. Show pictures. Create images. Give people the information to back up WHY you have a million dollar opportunity. WHY you have an opportunity that will fulfill any financial dream they may have.

NEW TREND - Prosperity

I spotted a new trend in Asia. An interesting change.
For years our industry has talked about the goal of creating 'financial freedom.' Earning enough money so that you can be free of money worries. This was presented with images of big houses, fast cars, yachts and other symbols of wealth. It was a very American concept.
In Asia, I have noticed a different vision of wealth. What I would call 'prosperity'. Asian wealth is not a personal or selfish concept; it involves all aspects of your life. Family, friends, health, spirituality, mental well-being and, of course, financial strength. It does not conflict with the 'Talk Cash' concept.
Prosperity is perceived as being created through co-operation, not conflict. Through teamwork, not through the singular efforts of one tough 'cowboy-like' entrepreneur.

Lesson Two

You need total commitment to create a FULL TIME attitude

When it comes to making your breakfast of bacon and eggs, who was more committed, the chicken or the pig?
The pig, of course.
The chicken was 'interested' yet the pig was fully committed.

Commitment to starting any venture is vital. You have to push as hard as you can to make sure you succeed. It does not matter what you are describing from education to wars. The committed succeed. The 'interested' fail.

Across the world, Network Marketing is presented as a great 'part-time' source of income. We pride ourselves on being able to deliver an excellent yet flexible income.
'When should I leave my job and go full-time?' Many people ask as they are sick of their jobs and excited.
The answer normally given?
'Wait until your network income exceeds your normal income for three consecutive months. That is the safe thing to do.'
How long is that?
'Maybe one to three years.'
Good advice? Sound conservative advice? Most people think so. Not in Asia!

The Asian Difference

It is not surprising that in Asia they have a different view. They believe in the potential of the industry. They know this is a once in a lifetime opportunity. Something to be grasped now.
People go FULL-TIME immediately.

Industry experts I have worked with estimate that there are on average 250,000 full-time networkers in countries such as Taiwan, Korea, Japan and Malaysia.
To put this in perspective. There are probably less than 250,000 full-time networkers in all of Europe.

Is it any surprise they grow so quickly when so many people are 100% focused on the business for their income?
This focus and commitment obviously breeds massive action. It breeds professionalism. It breeds enthusiasm. This all feeds through into results.
FAST RESULTS.
Fast Big Incomes feed the beliefs that you can make money in this business. The 'Get Rich Quick' dream that people have, it drives expectations up, it drives more people to work full-time.

So why isn't the rest of the world taking this FULL TIME attitude?

I see millions of people start their own business, buy a franchise or work in commission-only jobs FULL-TIME from the start. The insurance, advertising and real-estate industries would collapse if people were not prepared to risk FULL-TIME effort in their commission-only career. Why hasn't this attitude been employed towards Network Marketing?

The reason is simply the negative attitude.

Unfortunately, too many people promoting the industry have learnt negative attitudes from their parents, friends, schools and the media.

These attitudes are camouflaged in statements such as 'I am just being conservative'. It has developed an attitude where '*it is better to have not tried, than to have tried and failed.*' The fear of failure has over-powered any joy in success.

Conclusion

Am I saying that everyone should be full-time from day one? [I want to say 'YES yet......] Of course not.

What is needed is the FULL-TIME attitude.

That 100% passionate commitment that comes from people who HAVE TO succeed because they have burned all their bridges and have to succeed. What have you got to lose? [A better question] What have you got to gain?

What commitment is acceptable?

I can tell you that if you were sponsored by me into your business, I would expect 100% commitment from you.

I would expect you to invest every minute outside the time you HAD to give to your work, family and other vital commitments. Everything else MUST be spent on the business efforts we agreed for that critical early period. If you did not agree to this, I would ask that you joined another team.

This commitment is a test for me. It is a test to see how much you REALLY BELIEVE in our business. Those with weak beliefs will always struggle with the extra effort of starting a new opportunity. They will fall prey to the negative comments of people amongst them [even when the comments are from ignorant, scared, weak people.]

Am I being tough?

I hope so. You cannot put enough effort into your business in the first 90 days.

Masters Lesson

Get committed!
Go FULL TIME!

Lesson Three

You must form win-win relationships

Japan is a Network Marketing phenomenon.
With US$22 billion in annual sales and two million people involved, no country even comes close to Japan in terms of sales per person. When foreign companies launch Japan, the executives are amazed by the sheer speed and size of business created. The success dwarfs all other Asian countries.
Why is this so?
I found the answer to this question so enlightening and obvious that, if you will allow me, I will explain a cultural flaw most people suffer from and how the Japanese have overcome this to help create their global success story. It reveals an important lesson for all of us.

The cost of development

It is my opinion that modern, especially western, societies have ignored key fundamentals of human existence in their pursuit of individual development. For fifty years, we have championed individual opportunity and exploited technology to enhance our individual lifestyle. The results in terms of longevity, comfort and wealth are incredible.

If you remember the Taoist principle of opposites, you will therefore understand that the more we focus on one thing the more powerful the opposite becomes. Thus the more we have focused on individual freedom, the more communities have fallen apart.

Families are weak, local communities are weak, organizations are weak. Divorce, neglect, alienation are at record levels.

After fifty years of pursuing selfish goals, we can now see the costs of this pursuit in our everyday life.

It is not surprising that anxiety and fear are at record levels. Is it surprising are that people feel less happy today than they did 10, 20, 30 years ago? We have quantity of life without quality of life!

Network Marketing is probably the most humanistic business in the world. The company deals with most of the technical and administrative areas: your job is 99% involved with people. Talking to people.

Presenting to people.

Coaching and leading people.

As it is a business of volunteers [unlike an army or job], people tend to reflect the predominating attitudes in society. Network Marketing has naturally become a mirror of society.

Why the long philosophical speech?

Network Marketing is a 'people helping people' business. Unfortunately, most people DO NOT have this community value. Society has kicked the 'help people to help yourself' attitude out of them. We are selfish. Parents, teachers, commentators preach the mantra that you have to 'look after number one to survive!'

Thus many people struggle in Network Marketing simply because they are too selfish. They do not believe that the 'help others to help yourself' concept will work. They may poetically preach to you about how they will help you YET most people will not.

Why are the Japanese different?

Japan is a very homogenous society with 95% of people from Japanese heritage. This is a fiercely proud ancient race of people. For these reasons, foreign influences have had less impact on the Japanese culture. The country and society have retained many of their ancient values.

Influenced by their geography and large population, Japan, probably more than any other culture in the world, has had to develop values fundamental to living closely with other people. Thus they are famous for their politeness, quiet nature and willingness to work together.

For decades, Japanese companies have worked together as partners in a way unmatched in any other country.
The Japanese have learnt that to win in the long term; The team will always beat the individual.
They strongly believe that if the strong help the weak, the strong will grow stronger. They believe that long term success is based on win-win relationships between people and corporations.
Success is based on relationships so if your partner fails, you fail. You will lose respect in a nation where respect is often considered more important than life itself.

Can you see how his will have impacted on Network Marketing?
It means that if I sponsor you, I am GUARANTEEING you [based on my all-important credibility] that I will help you succeed. EVEN if this means I will fail. I have become your 'servant-leader'.
Importantly, it also obliges you, due to the strong 'master-pupil' attitude in Japan, to do as we agree.
Together we become a team who have committed ourselves in the strongest way to work together for everyone's benefit.
We all win because we all work together.
The experienced must teach and support the new and under-confident.
The new must follow the advice of the experienced.
Together we become a team.

Put these attitudes in a company and you can also see how bureaucracy could reign in some Japanese organizations. How failing companies or ineffective employees could be supported for years as has happened over the last decade in Japan.
YET apply these attitudes in a people business like Network Marketing and the power of the system is released. It is enhanced. People helping people succeed.

Master's lesson

Whatever level you are in this business, learn this critical lesson from the Japanese masters. Only create win-win relationships with your people.

Advice

Most people do not believe in teamwork. They are brainwashed in this selfish attitude of the new world YET they want to be part of a relationship.
They want to believe that working together will be more successful.
So sit down with all new people in your team and lay out clearly what the expectations are of each other; what will each do to ensure their success. Then deliver on your part of the agreement. If they do not, then you know they are not worth dealing with so move on to helping someone else.

Lesson Four

Everybody needs to hear about the opportunity as soon as possible

Share your knowledge, it's the only way to achieve immortality
Dalai Lama

Marie was the top leader in the Philippines and she introduced her team to me, 'this is my sister, my sister, my brother and my mother.' Welcome to 'A Family Affair!'
In Asia, family and friends are everything. Thus when a person joins a networking business, the FIRST people they talk to are those they have the closest relationship to.

If you want to create a TidalWave! then you need to recruit lots of people as fast as possible.
This means you need to talk to lots of people.
EVERYONE you know and meet.
As FAST as you can.
Family and friends FIRST.
If you see a good movie, go to a great restaurant, the first people you tell are your friends and family. You want to share the news which means you are also advertising for the movie company or restaurant.
Do you care?
Of course not. They are not paying for your advertising their business or product.

It therefore seems sensible that the first people you should tell about your new networking business are your friends and family.
If you do not, then you need to think clearly about either your business or your relationships.
If you do not believe in the potential of the business then you will never be motivated to succeed. Go back to your sponsor and re-associate yourself with the potential of the opportunity. Then back to family and friends.

Win-win

Remember the Japanese win-win relationship? This is the attitude with your friends and family. Together you take out the risks and concerns.

Credibility problems

If you do not want to tell your friends and family first then you must have either poor relationships or you feel that you lack the credibility to present a business opportunity to them.
What right have you got to offer a business opportunity to your successful uncle, dynamic friend or ambitious sister? Especially if you have no record of success in business!
Will they laugh at you?
Will you be responsible for their success?
My experience is that most people will not approach their

friends and family because of some credibility or responsibility issue. They miss out on their easiest prospective new recruits! I have known countless examples of best friends, family, even brothers, ending up in different networks in the same company just because the first person who joined did not approach the other!

What is your Job?

Your job is simply to offer the business opportunity to everyone in the same enthusiastic manner. It is not your job to decide if they are going to join, that's their choice. Their decision. Their responsibility.
If a friend or family member joined then great. You have someone you know to share the business talk with. Someone else who is connected with the future of the business.

Sharpshooter or shotgun?

When you join a network business, you have a short period of time to make an impact. When your enthusiasm levels are at their highest. At this time, people will feel your excitement. They will be inspired by it. It will probably be the most important determinant of them joining your business.
The question on many people's lips is ***'Should I be selective***

about who I talk to?'
Become the 'sharpshooter'. Headhunt the best people?
It is a topic of intense debate by some people and my answer is definitely 'NO!'
I have seen more people become successful because they adopted the 'shotgun' approach and talked to everyone immediately rather than those that try to be selective.
Who knows who will want to join you in your business?
Who knows what is going on in the minds of the people you know and meet?
The happiest looking people maybe the most frustrated and sad. Most uninspired non-active people are just looking for something to turn them on!

Asian Masters

They talk to everyone. Everyone. Immediately.
When I have had evening meetings launching companies, after the meeting, people will call their friends and arrange for them to meet me or the company executives at our hotel that night! People will be brought to the hotel past midnight. Breakfast meetings will be arranged. They talk to everyone immediately.

It is this attitude of 'lets talk to everyone immediately' that makes a huge difference. People buy people. They are more interested in how you feel about the opportunity than the detail of the opportunity. If you are hugely enthusiastic, then they will risk joining just to be as enthusiastic as you are. This is the fire that drives the initial months of your business. This is the fire that gets your new team of people working. You can create this fire, which is why I know you can be successful in this business. To create a TidalWave!

Master's Lesson

Talk to everybody once you have completed your Quick Start training. 24/7. No stopping. Practice will make your presentations better. Always family and friends first.

Lesson Five

Understanding creates the confidence to act with pride

'You please sign, Mr Ludbrook', he said as he pushed his hand-written notes on our conversation in front of me. I looked at him in surprise. No-one had ever asked me to sign the notes of a meeting.
The other Chinese leaders were smiling at me. My interpreter and client nodded as if this was normal and expected. They wanted to know I was sure of the details. Such are the Asian Masters, meticulous when it comes to the detail of the business.

Confusion is the cancer of the networking business.
Confused people do nothing. They just wait to be 'unconfused'.
Most new people fail because they are confused about what they need to do and what are the possible rewards.
Across Asia I have noticed that they always want to know the facts of the business. AND they want proof. If you claim the product has a 'patent pending', they want to see the actual paperwork of the patent. If you claim a product is made a certain way, they want to see pictures of this process.
Are they distrustful?...No!
Are they creating more confusion?.... No!
I think it is very smart.
It creates total understanding of the basic business model.

They want to know and will KEEP asking questions until they understand. Questions like:
How does the Compensation Plan work? How do they get to the key levels in the fastest way with the least work?
How do I order? What is the cost? What is the best size order? When is training?
Questions, questions.
All of the basic questions that a new person should know to ask if they want to be successful.
PLEASE NOTE. Once they have the important facts about the plans, claims and credibility of the company, products and business programme, they do not keep asking for more information. They act!

Confidence! Belief!

Understanding creates confidence. Written proof creates belief in the business. It feeds motivation. Can you see how this emphasis on understanding in the initial stage actually accelerates growth?

Time to learn?

How long will they spend understanding the business? Asking for proof? Weeks? Days? If they get the facts immediately, they will take hours. They will try to understand the key points as soon as possible.

The Master's Lesson

You must know what you are expected to do to reach the first STABLE level of leadership. This is not normally the first leadership position in your Compensation Plan. It is the position where you have to prove that you have a structured network AND enough volume for you to earn an attractive income. An income that it would be difficult to walk away from.
If there are any claims you are confused about and do not believe then ask for proof. You may receive a negative response from your upline [they may not have the proof]. Yet persist, as unless you receive a clear answer, this concern will always hold you back.

With proof, you then have every reason to go into 100% Action!

Say it with Pride

Ask many people in Network Marketing what they do and they will mumble some confusing statement looking very embarrassed. The questioner will register the embarrassment and assume that you are either lying or doing something illegal. Is this you?

Ask a doctor, farmer, banker or student what they do and the answer is clear. So what is the problem?

- Don't know what this business is?
- Do you think that you're doing something illegal, immoral, unethical?
- Worried someone will laugh or ridicule you?
- Don't know what to say?

Why is this important?

We are in the marketing business. Our job is to advertise to people that we have a great financial opportunity. New people often struggle with an answer to this initial question **'what do you do?'**

You need an answer. Simple, clear and obvious.

What do they say in Asia?

There was no standard magic saying for you to use. Everyone uses something different. What I did notice was more important than any word uttered. The Asians are proud to be in this business. They are excited about it. You can see it in their eyes and hear it in their voices.

Everywhere I have traveled in Asia, I have seen people with their company pins on. Ask them what they do and they say 'I am in Network Marketing'. With a smile on their face. With a glint in their eye. With pride. It is inspiring. You want to know more about it.

What else do they do?

Not only did they wear their company recognition pins. You can see them carrying company bags, company clothes, with company stickers on their cars. They are proud of their business.

They revealed a pride and excitement about their company that I only see in those that work for the huge global companies like Coca-cola, Shell and Sony.

This pride and raw enthusiasm obviously shines through their presentations. In their prospecting. Never forget 'people buy people'. By showing this pride they make their opportunity valuable.

Master's Lesson

Make sure you learn the facts. Not everything about everything just what your sponsor advises you need to know.

Most importantly, learn about your company, its future, its successes so you can have absolute pride and confidence.

Rapid action creates rapid results.

Like a steam train, motivation is purely steam unless you can put it through your engine to create action.

Lesson Six

At the start, 24/7 effort is the minimum

This lesson is obvious. The harder you work, the quicker you learn, the more results you will produce.
No-one works harder than the Asian Masters when they start a new network - 24 hours a day, 7 days a week - 24/7.

Is it tiring?

At the time, you do not notice the work hours because it is so much fun. They are excited. They are enthusiastic. So you do not get tired until you leave.
For me, its always crazy work.
They want breakfast meetings, tea meetings, lunch, dinner and after dinner meetings. To introduce new people to you. To find out the best ways to grow fast. To learn more about the products, company and vision to help them become more effective.

Have you ever worked extremely hard yet didn't feel tired because you were having so much fun?
That's how it feels working with 24/7 motivated people! Their enthusiasm drives you on.

Why is this important?

Remember the TidalWave! principle in building a network. You have joined a company and your goal is to create momentum in your network as fast as possible. Just like getting an airplane airborne, the biggest energy is at the start. Once you are flying, it is much easier.

You do this working your Quick Start [or whatever it is called] programme. What I call the ***Flywheel***. You are sponsoring and coaching as fast as possible until your business grows without you.

Maximum effort - 24/7

No motivation

The only reason you will not work 24/7 is your motivation. If you are totally charged up, you will work every hour that you have spare. You will make time. You will cancel previous engagements. Your social life will be put on hold.

I can hear people groan.

Quite frankly, you will gladly focus 100% of the time on your business if you are motivated. Your negative attitude towards missing your favourite TV show, weekly golf game, a shopping trip or Sunday afternoon sleep is purely because you have not tapped into the excitement of your business.

Motivate yourself NOW

You cannot be TOO motivated. Most are only about 20% motivated. They smile and think they are enthusiastic. Not good enough!

To work the hardest, to truly influence people with your excitement, you must have EXCESS enthusiasm. That's enough to make steam come out of your ears AND enough to charge up other people.

How do you motivate yourself to a state of white hot excitement?

1. What is the future of the industry?

Are you in the right industry at the right time? Is this a boom industry? Why?

This is a much more important question than you think. It is the bedrock of this opportunity. It will also help you discuss this industry with more educated prospective distributors. Read **'Shakeout! The Big Picture'** book.

2. What is the future of your company?

Find out some facts and basic strategies. Where are they expanding to? New countries. New products. What is your competitive edge? Why are you the best at what you do? Get associated with your business so you can explain it to anyone.

3. Your Lifestyle Story.

This is **your greatest motivator**. All great leaders have great personal stories on 'why they joined their company and what is their hope for the future. What lifestyle they dream of? It should inspire and excite you every time you say it. If you are new, you should be telling this story to everyone. It is your most powerful Sponsoring tool.

4. Other testimonials

Collect the Success stories of other people. Let them inspire you. Build your belief.

5. What are your short term goals? Next 7 days?

6. What is your plan?

7. There are great books to read. Speakers to listen to.

8. EVENTS, EVENTS, EVENTS.

Going to all events should be compulsory. They are so important, no excuse is acceptable.

Use everything

Motivation and attitude change is so important at the start of this business. It is hard to motivate yourself in a negative world. With effort, you can achieve a state of EXCESS enthusiasm. Enthusiasm which does not repel, it inspires people. Enthusiasm which acts like a magnet, drawing people to you.
Everyone has this ability in themselves. It makes ugly people pretty. It makes tired people dance. You cannot work enough on creating enthusiasm in your life.

Master's Lesson

Live it for 1 year

I chanced upon one of these online IQ tests which always catch me. After doing the test and filling out their personal information form, I had to wait for their calculation of my IQ. Whilst this was calculating, they informed me that I had lived for 2,155 weeks! Here was I worrying about getting a book finished this week when I had already lived for 2,155 weeks!
Give this business one year to work. Live it. Experience all of the joys and sorrows of one year. 52 weeks. This is such a short time in your life and you know you have to give this opportunity a chance to change your life for the better.

Lesson Seven

Unquestionably follow the coaching of your Upline

An ancient Japanese story tells of the new monk arriving at the temple and talking enthusiastically with the old master. The old master suggests that they have some tea and starts to fill the student's cup. To the students great alarm, the master fills the cup yet does not stop pouring and tea spills all over the ground.
The master tells the student 'You will not be studying here yet. You are like this cup, your mind is so full that nothing else will go in. Go away and clear your mind so you can learn what is important.'

All over the world, new people start our business with a mind full of how they will succeed. They receive the business system, designed by experts, and the first thing they do is try and change it! Crazy! Or, even worse, just ignore it! They question or ignore the coaching of their sponsors and Upline. People with experience.

Throughout Asia I found a deferential attitude between new people and their Upline. There was respect. There was acceptance of advice.

I found that new people naturally assumed a student role and did not question what was being asked of them. They assumed that their Upline was more knowledgeable and more experienced and thus their directions were the best course of action. They did not try to introduce new methods, systems or strategies.

What a smart strategy!

Too often I see people in Europe, new people, assuming that they know better than their more experienced Uplines. They challenge the strategies offered. They doubt the intentions of the most successful people. The result is confusion and half-hearted action resulting in poor performance.

Initiative and originality is a great asset in designers and leaders. It is not useful in the first wave of Network Marketing when the strategy is for EVERYONE to follow the same system to allow for the duplication of efforts. You cannot duplicate originality, only systems!

You cannot duplicate originality, only systems!

A lesson from the world's best.

Think of the McDonalds restaurant franchise. The most successful business system in the world. It does not matter who you were before you bought a McDonalds franchise, you are NEVER EVER allowed to change the system. Do their system differently and they will remove it from you.

Everyone needs mentors

I think television, films, music and the schools have created an attitude of challenging any authority. Of challenging advice given. Of rejecting wisdom.
Perhaps it is our changing world where top CEO's can be 35 years old. Wisdom is being discounted against ability to act in a changing world. Wisdom is not as valued as it used to be.

Network Marketing is based on systems that should not change. This is why wisdom is valuable. This is why mentors are so valuable. This why your Upline can be so valuable especially when you are younger.
The Asian culture admires youthful success yet respects

wisdom and the importance of respect. I can see it throughout the networks as the new people [whatever their age] seek and follow the advice of the more successful. Those with success take on the role of mentor very seriously. They see it as an honour that comes with responsibility. The advice and support they must give is important and must be right.

Master's Lesson

Sit down with everyone who joins your team and make them read this chapter. It will save them and you days of heartbreak. Be direct with them. Tell them what they should do. When they start doing the wrong thing, tell them not to. Do not be vague or confusing.

Lesson Eight

Reward and recognise as much as possible

It was a lovely tropical night in the Philippines. I was the guest of honour at a conference held in a hotel complex in the old American Clark Air Base, once the largest airforce base in Asia. This was a typically Asian event; it was a recognition carnival. There were certificates awarded. Pins, medals and sashes presented. Cash given away. People were presented with flowers, gifts and travel incentives. Everyone, even the newest person, came away feeling they were a winner.

Then the photos started....as the guest of honour, I must have had 100 different photos taken of me with people. Around me ten times more photos were taken. My face ached from smiling.

Then there was the entertainment. Teams of people had prepared dances and small plays reflecting the fun they had in the business. Most were very humorous.

The lessons here are important

Think about your first 3-6 month in your business. Are you going to make a lot of money? It is possible yet not normal; this is the building phase. Thus the most important job of your Upline support team is to keep you motivated. To build your spirits.

This is what they were doing this evening and I find that

the Asians are Masters at recognizing success. They are masters at building enthusiasm, fun and teamwork in their people. Even the newest least confident person is involved and actively participates in building the passion in the team.

Master's Lessons

1. Actively use any recognition of your people. Do not limit yourself to your teams recognition. Add your own awards of things such as flowers and certificates.
2. Use photos of your team to help you build your team.
3. Get photos of you and your team with any top people, speaker or company executive to help in your presentations. Your prospects will be impressed.
4. Have fun events

Personal TidalWave!

I hope you want to get rich quick. The formula is simple:

1. **Join the right industry**
2. **Join at the right time**
3. **Be in the right company**
4. **Take massive action**

I am sure that the first three points are already in place, now its time to follow the next two. In Networking, your job is to create a TidalWave!

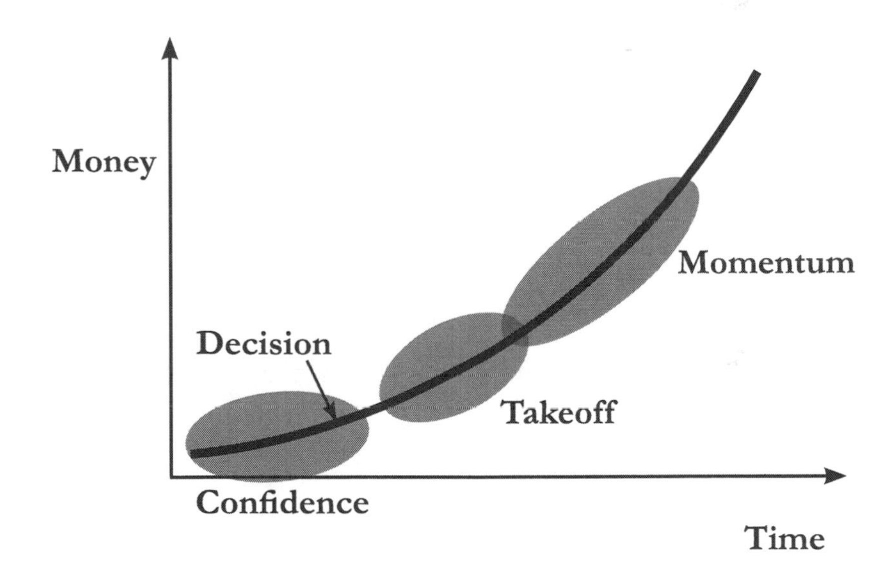

The TidalWave!

You need to put a massive 24/7, 110% FULLTIME effort in at the start to create the momentum in your network so that it grows without you. So your team has the motivation and performance to keep working on their own and as a team.
Are you going to make a lot of mistakes?
Yes
Are you going to have tough days?
Yes
Will you want to know everything?
Yes

YET the key to success is going into massive action with just the basics in mind. Your focus needs to be on creating EXCESS ENTHUSIASM so people are attracted to your excitement. They are inspired by your story and efforts.

The Asian Masters are producing incredible results yet they are not using unique strategies and do not possess unique skills. They do the Basics uniquely well. They just do the same things that you are coached to do and their lessons for you are clear:

Lesson One	You need to explain a huge future that inspires massive action immediately
Lesson Two	You need total commitment to create a FULL TIME attitude

Lesson Three	You must form win-win relationships
Lesson Four	Everybody needs to hear about the opportunity as soon as possible
Lesson Five	Understanding creates the confidence to act with pride
Lesson Six	At the start, 24/7 effort is the minimum
Lesson Seven	Unquestionably follow the coaching of your Upline
Lesson Eight	Reward and recognise as much as possible

Learn and live these lessons and you will create your own Personal TidalWave! it will create a network in momentum. That network is the base for a lifelong residual income. A lifestyle of your dreams. A bigger, better, stronger you.
Obviously, you need to learn new skills and one day master the leadership skills necessary to influence your network. First things first! You need to build a network to lead first. In the TAKE OFF period you must put in all the effort you can. 110%, 24/7 FULLTIME.
The reward is a TidalWave! the base for a never-ending income.
The key to Getting Rich Quickly.

Good luck

ABOUT EDWARD

The Network Coach

Ed has a unique role in the global Network Marketing industry as a Network Coach and has coached over 100 organisations and 100,000's of people across the world since 1994. He is Europe's leading author and speaker on Network Marketing who has sold over 2 million books in 20 languages.

For 15 years, Ed has been pioneering competence-based [100% Success] training systems with Network Marketing. He is passionate about the delivering significantly higher success rates because it will transform this industry and empower everyone involved to achieve their dreams. He presents the 100% Success TV show [www.100percentsuccess.tv] to entertain and educate people in dynamic 5 minute shows.

Ed's true passion is Leadership training and he has trained Network Leaders across the world for many years. Due to the normal leadership approaches not being effective in this unique Network environment, he developed the 100% Leadership approach. His leadership blog is www.100percentleadership.com

Raised in New Zealand, Edward graduated from Royal Military College Duntroon, Australia's prestigious army officer university. He served in the NZ Army Engineers then moved to London where he worked in investment banking and strategic consultancy before focusing on the Network Marketing industry.

When the industry has embraced his 100% Success vision based on the core concepts of competence based learning and leadership he intends to retire, help save the planet from global warming and produce a fantastic Rose wine to celebrate life with his family in the sun.

To hire Ed as the keynote speaker at your next conference, email his office on admin@ludbrook.com